FOCUS

Productive Leadership in Action

WTL PRESS

Ashley M. Martin

FOCUS
Productive Leadership In Action

© Original Publication Date. 2014 Updated 2017.

Published in Houston, Texas, by WTL Press.

Books may be purchased in bulk for educational, business, fund-raising, or sales promotional use. For more information, please e-mail info@iamashleym.com.

Unless otherwise noted, scriptures taken from the New King James Version®. Copyright © 1982 by Thomas Nelson. Used by permission. All rights reserved.

Library of Congress has cataloged this edition as follows
Focus: Productive Leadership in Action / Ashley Martin

Library of Congress Control Number: 2017912634

ISBN: 978-0-9907701-4-5

Printed in the United States of America

i

Dedication

To my parents,
Frank and Deborah Martin

Thank you for your invaluable deposits and solid
foundation. I am because you are.
Expect a great return on your investments – tangible and
intangible.

FOCUS
Productive Leadership In Action

Preface

Continual improvement in life is a must. The first edition of Focus: A Handbook for Leaders was published in 2014. Life experiences shifted the author's perspective and motivations. Feedback from readers was given and received. The result is this 2nd edition of the book, *Focus: Productive Leadership in Action.*

Introduction

The apple red bow wrapped around the big rectangular box called my name everyday leading up to Christmas. Every time I passed the Christmas tree, it was as if the present called my name "Ashley, come here. Do you want to see what's in the box?" What excited 9-year-old would not want to see what was in a beautifully wrapped box with their name on it. Unwisely and naively, I listened to it. Every day I turned the box over and began to peel back the wrapping paper to get a sneak peek into my gift.

"I wonder whose little fingers have been peeling away the wrapping paper." My mother's words struck a cord in my body. All I could think about was the fact that she knew I had been tearing the wrapping paper. Ashley," she called. "Yes," I answered back, nervous that she found out my secret.

As I walked over to her by the Christmas tree, I was unnerved. "Come and see something," she said. "What is it?" I said pretending not to know anything and hoping that she did not find out that I had been sneaking by the Christmas tree every day since she put the gift out there.

"Something has been nibbling at one of your gifts."

"Really?" I asked ready to receive the inevitable scolding.

"Yep," she replied. "Guess, I'm going to have to put it away until Christmas day so that it doesn't become completely undone." With a chuckle in her voice and smile on her face, she whisked the gift away into hiding until Christmas day.

I was relieved yet annoyed that I was not going to be able to continue my sneak peek. In addition to learning how to handle a situation gracefully as my mother did, I learned the importance of patience and what I should be doing when it came to getting what I desired. After a few more days of good behavior, I was going to have the very thing I wanted in my hands.

Reflecting on this childhood memory made me realize how often we adults still get distracted on the wrong things and fail to focus on the right things when it comes to obtaining a desire or reaching a goal. All I was tasked with doing was focusing on and committing to the productive tasks– my chores and school work- and ultimately, I would receive my gift. I was distracted by the wrapping paper, that charming red bow, and the thought of that gift being all mine.

Most adults may agree that distractions do not go away as you grow. In fact, I would dare to say that they increase as you age. However true this may be, there are ways to handle them.

George Lucas boldly states that your focus determines your reality. I agree one hundred percent with him. Where your focus goes, the rest flows. It is an easy and simple concept yet for several reasons this can be a challenge for many in today's distracted society.

We are constantly bombarded with distractions. The latest politics and events of the world, technology, life's circumstances, our relationships, and even our own racing thoughts all vie for our attention. While all these things are important, I would imagine that you too sometimes need help to get and stay focused. In the midst of the beautiful chaos that is life, there are intentional things that can be done to create focus in your life and get on the road to seeing your goals manifested.

Defining Focus

For the purpose of this book and to keep things simple, focus will be defined in two contexts - as a noun (thing) and as a verb (action).

Focus defined as a noun is twofold.

a. Maximum clarity of an idea
b. The concentration of attention or energy on something

Focused defined in terms of a verb is two-fold.

a. To direct your attention on something
b. To bring into alignment

4

You cannot have one without the other. **Focus (the thing) is only as effective as your ability to bring things into focus through ACTION.** Another way to simplify the concept of focus is with this acronym.

Fixed
On
Course
Until
Successful

What's So Special About Focus?

Passion, drive, determination, and vision are major keys to reaching goals; however, focus and the benefits that come with it are often overlooked and equally as important as the other principle.

No matter whom you are or where you are, distractions will arise. It is a part of the fabric of our society. From group texts to pop ups on the computer to the phone ringing, distractions are at an all-time high and comes with the territory of the times we are living in.

There may be times when your passion level is low or you simply just don't feel like it. You may be going through the motions or may be hanging on by a thread. Moments like these call for focus.

Steve Jobs: An Example of Focus

" "That's been one of my mantras-focus and simplicity. Simple can be harder than complex; You have to work hard to get your thinking clean to make it simple. But it's worth it in the end because once you get there, you can move mountains."

- Steve Jobs

Steve Jobs, the mastermind and creative visionary behind Apple, is a prime example of the power of focus. His efforts produced the Apple computer, Mac laptops, iPod, iPhone, and Pixar Animation Studios. These products and services have revolutionized how our society - our communication, entertainment, and productivity.

I am convinced that the power of focus allowed Jobs to pioneer these innovations. Jobs had a compelling vision to get computers into the hands of everyday people. He had a unique leadership aesthetic and way of thinking. Ultimately, he knew the strategy of focus would lead him to success.

It was through unlikely circumstances that we witness one of the way Steve Jobs understood and applied the principle of focus. In 1997, Jobs returned to Apple after being fired (from the company he started). Apple's quarterly sales were down by 30 percent. They were on the brink of failure.

In an attempt to understand the company's problems, Jobs posed a question to his managers about the company's products. "Which product should I tell my friends about?" I could be wrong but my interpretation was that he wanted to gauge what their best products were. No one in the room could produce a simple answer. I imagine that the room may have been filled with blank stares and silence.

The lack of simplicity in their responses compelled him to reduce the number of products Apple was selling by 70 percent. They would focus on four products– two types of desktop computers and two types of laptops. When explaining his decision to reduce the product line, Jobs affirmed, **"deciding what not to do is as important as deciding what to do."**

Within two years, Apple turned what seemed to be a business disaster into a $300 million-dollar profit machine. **Jobs' ability to create a focused environment was crucial to Apple's success.**

Jobs understood that focus gives meaningful direction and fosters simplicity. It allows individuals to build on their strengths. The mastery of one thing makes for a greater sense of accomplishment. Likewise, when an organization focuses on fewer goals with greater impact

7

over many, they may do a better job of honing their efforts and attention. Less truly is more.

On the other hand, the opposite of focus is what I describe as being "all over the place." Lack of organization, cohesiveness, and direction are all symptoms of being all over the place. Before Jobs' return to Apple in 1997, Apple's line of products was in this state. The dozens of items they were selling led to unbeneficial distractions and a disorganized vision. His commitment to reduce the quantity and upgrade the quality proved to be a winning decision for the company.

It Starts with You and Keeps Going

It is possible to experience the turn around and success Apple has. While you are not Steve Jobs, you are the mastermind and visionary of your own life and organization –if you lead one. You can apply focus to your life.

I am a living witness to the benefits to what the power of focus can do in your life. There is no guarantee that everything will work for you as it has for Steve Jobs or even myself, but it with hopes that some of the tools and strategies offered can assist in transform your life in a way that is more productive and help your goals.

If you are the leader of an organization, the principle of focus can work at all levels of your organization; however, it all starts with you. You are the captain steering the ship and with that comes a responsibility to keep not only yourself but others on track. Having served in several leadership capacities in educational and non-profit settings taught me the importance of putting focus into practice. A focused leader has a greater likelihood to create a productive environment where people flourish and goals are met.

In order to see the power of focus at work in your life as you pursue goals, some key initial components are needed. They include:

- Vision – a mental picture for the future
- Knowing and articulating your why
- Knowing and developing the person in the mirror
- Knowing and developing the people on the journey with you
- A good mix of courage, discipline, a plan, and action.

There are some other strategies and tools outlined in this book to help you put the power of focus to work. Before you get started, I would like to offer some suggestions for how to digest the content.

Focus on one chapter at a time. There are some complimentary chapters. Chew on the nuggets of information that speak to you or those on the journey with you.

Read in a focused environment. Find a space where you can fully engage in reading. It may be your favorite coffee shop, chair, or park bench. Wherever it is, make sure it is peaceful and conducive to your learning and easily absorbing information.

Implement at least one "reflect and act" per chapter. Start small with one strategy and then expand.

Be truthful, transparent, and reflective. Be honest with yourself. True transformation and improvement occurs when we are brutally honest with ourselves about where we are and where we want to be. As you read, consider where you can apply the information to you first and then to those in your organization.

Remember, where your focus goes, the rest flows. Focus is the key to productive leadership. Let's get focused!

Part I: The Basics

Focus & Your Brain

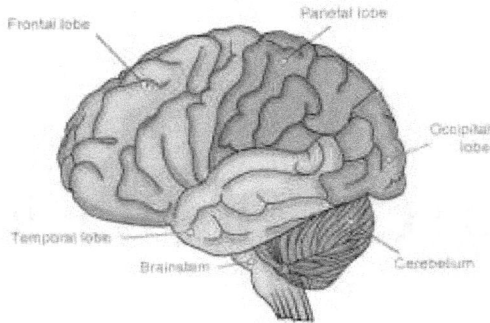

i

While one could argue that the entire brain is responsible for your ability to focus, there are areas primarily used for focus - the frontal lobe, parietal lobe, and brainstem. Chemicals, neurotransmitters, and hormones also factor into our ability to stay "in the zone."

When it comes to the brain, there are two types of attention grabbers. First, there are intentional attention-grabbers. You give your attention to these things on purpose like reading this book or you are watching your favorite TV show. In contrast, there are distractions. Often uninvited, these attention grabbers seemingly pop out of nowhere and interrupt your focus. Distractions can be defined as such.

1. The act of distracting or the condition of being distracted

2. Something that makes it difficult to pay attention or that draws attention away from familiar or everyday concerns.

3. Mental or emotional disturbance; agitation or confusion

In *Your Brain at Work*, author David Rock states that distractions tell the brain that something has changed. They are an alert saying, "Hey you! Look at me. I may be dangerous or delightful." Simply put, a distraction is something that takes your attention off something you were concentrated on.

I confess that sparkly things have had a tendency to get my attention. With advances in science and technology, it is very easy to get off course from something you were concentrating on. Before moving forward, I do want to mention that not all interruptions are bad. A few "good" distractions include your light bulb moments, intentional shifts when you need a brain break, or interruptions when you need to get your mind off of something that you should not be thinking about.

Internal Distractions

The mind is a constant battlefield. The voices in your head can help or hinder you! The messages floating around constantly bombard us. Just as there are things that can feed or fuel your focus, negativity, doubt, frustration, anger, along with a litany of other negative responses, can pull individuals away from their focus.

You may have experienced this before. You want to move forward with something but right before you do something creeps in. They sound like this. "That's crazy. You're wasting your time. You can't do that." Ignoring those voices and moving forward is necessary for your success. Consider these tips in your effort to combat internal distractions.

Positive Affirmations

Words give life. Positive psychology shows the benefits of affirming yourself. There is nothing more beneficial than speaking positively about yourself. Remind yourself that you are great, you are thriving, you are a winner. Eventually, you will become what you say. Speak it, believe it, and you will see it. (Check out the reference section for a recommended product.)

Positive Mindset

"As a man thinketh, so is he." Where the mind goes, the rest flows. There is a tendency to become what and how you think about yourself. Think wisely and creatively. Feed your mind with information that will help you stay focused.

Positive Visuals

What you see matters! There is an entire portion of your brain dedicated to vision. Strategically position visuals that will help you. Vision boards and inspiring paintings are a few examples of the visuals that can combat internal distractions.

Professional Help

Occasionally there is a need for professional assistance in combating distracting thoughts. This is totally okay. There are many professionals equipped to help you succeed.

External Distractions

External distractions are outside attention-grabbers that surround us. They come in the form of people, environments, and habits constantly bombard our brains, shouting at us, "Hey you! Look at me."

People distractions are real and are out there. Have you ever been out somewhere and a debonair dude or beautiful lady walks your way? All of a sudden, your attention shifts and your head turns. That visual stimulus has distracted you from what you were doing or thinking. Likewise, irritating, demanding, or overbearing people can distract us and get us off course.

Environment plays a major role in your ability to focus. Noise level, room temperature, decor, and the overall energy in a room matter. If you're like me, I need great lighting, a little bit of white noise or motivating music, and just the right temperature to be productive. Pay attention to what the conditions are like where you work the best. Just as people and environment can be distracting, habits can be distracting.

Technology has contributed greatly to our society, but it has also added to the bad **habits** that cause people to lose focus and feed culture- induced ADD. We text and drive. We text and walk – equally as dangerous. We check Facebook, Instagram, and Twitter while talking on the phone, and watching television. How is that possible? It sounds bizarre, but this is our reality.

By now, you may realize that you or someone you know could use some help focusing a little better. Don't feel bad. You are among the thousands that need help. Consider the simple process below for help minimizing and eliminating distractions.

Step 1: Identify your distraction.
• Is it internal, external, or both?

Step 2: Eliminate or minimize the distraction.
• If the negative thought comes, tell it to shut up. Replace it on a positive affirmation.
• If it is your electronics, consider silencing them.
• If someone needs you and it is not urgent or a priority, schedule an alternate time to talk.

Step 3: Carry on and focus on your work.
In addition to this simple process, there are proactive measures you can take to handle distractions for the long haul.

Proactive Focus Practices

C reate distraction free time. Take a ten-minute brain break in silence or mediate. There is a ton of research on the positive effects of mindfulness and meditation. These techniques help to quiet the busy mind and help you to become more aware on the present moment. In fact, research has found that mediation reduces cortisol levels (the stress hormone). It lowers the blood pressure and increases immune response (Pickert, 2014).

Reduce multi-tasking. Much research shows that multi-tasking reduces productivity. This may be a challenge for many, particularly we ladies who are used to multi-tasking. In his book, *Brain Rules*, John Medina, highlights that a person who is interrupted takes fifty percent longer to accomplish a task. In addition, he or she makes up to 50 % more errors.

Use checklists. Call it what you want, there is something incredibly gratifying about checking something off a to-do list. Make a list of your priorities and check them off as you go. Lists work!

Reward yourself after completing a task. This is self-explanatory. You finished your task! Grab the ice cream, bottle of wine, eat the cookie, or buy the shoes. It is a great habit to celebrate your accomplishments great and small.

Limit electronics while working on major tasks. Unless electronics are vital to completing tasks, designate times to check emails or take and return phone calls.

Pay attention to when and where you focus best. Try to do your most important tasks **when** (time of day) and **where (**setting) you focus best.

Is it early in the morning when you are fresh? Is late at night when all is quiet? Are you in the bedroom, office, or at the park? Set yourself up for success and conquer that work in the best setting.

Focus is a muscle that has to be exercised just like any other muscle in your body. As any trainer would probably tell you, start small and at your pace. From there, implement components to build up your focus muscles. Since most great transformations begin from the inside out, it is suggested that you start by conquering your internal distractions and then working towards conquering the external distractions.

Part II: The FOCUS Factor

The Beauty of Balance & Self-Care

"The key to gaining work-life balance is finding your life's rhythm and flow."

I regularly visit the chiropractor for adjustments. Many dismiss chiropractic care but it is a hidden jewel in preventative and restorative self - care. On my initial visit and consultation, I was told that one of my hips was slightly higher than the other. If you could have seen my facial expressions, you would have laughed. According to my chiropractor, I had been walking around imbalanced and did not even know it. I did not feel any different and everything was "normal" as far as I could tell. It was not until I finally started feeling the discomfort in my back and neck that I realized I needed to make some adjustments.

So often we operate like this in life. We hustle, bustle, and strive for "above and beyond" and working long hours is the norm. As workplace demands increase, the dialogue concerning proper work-life balance increases. Let's consider some current stats.

- In 2010, Strategy One conducted research that revealed that 89 percent of 1,043 Americans stated work- life balance was a problem in the United States.
- Fifty-four percent of those participants cited it as a "significant" problem.
- In 2015, the Harris Poll conducted a survey on behalf of Ernst & Young Global Limited that reported, approximately 46% of 9,699 managers globally are working more than 40 –hour weeks.
- 4 in 10 say their hours have increased over the past five years.

Try this brief self-assessment to gauge whether you are among the many that are concerned with work-life balance.

- Do you often stay at work late and/or bring work home?
- Do you need more rest on a daily basis?
- Is your schedule overbooked?
- Do you wish that you could spend more time with
- your family and friends or just by yourself?
- Do you often feel irritable, easily frustrated,
- stressed out, or burned out?

If you answered "yes" to a majority of these questions, then you are probably struggling and are out of balance.

An imbalance between your work and your personal life can take a toll on your body, family, career, spirit, and soul. It is easier than you think to get off balance. If you have been ambitious like I have been, it is extremely easy get out of balance. Eventually, it will not serve you well.

Having a proper work-life not only increases productivity but also inspires innovation. Balance helps you with problem solving, be more effective in reaching goals, and aids better decision making.

Establishing this highly sought-after balance and proper self-care is not as hard as it seems. How balance plays out in our lives looks varies from person to person, but there are some common threads. Knowing and establishing priorities, knowing your capacity, setting boundaries, and planning are all a part of the puzzle.

Priorities

Where do you invest the most time, energy, and money? This often tells the tale of what we deem as a priority. Simply put, a priority is something that is more important than the other. They can include but are not limited to our spirituality, relationships, and career. Let's take a deeper look.

Spiritual

In my humble opinion, the things unseen to the natural eye hold a lot of weight for what we see with flesh and blood. Ensuring that there is alignment internally is extremely important to me. Cultivating a relationship with the Creator is vital to my life. Whether it is through prayer, reading, and/or meditation, I value this time and consider it my life line and what keeps me centered. When I intentionally prioritize this component of my life, everything else in my life seems to flow. If you are feeling a bit out of whack or off balance, perhaps spirituality needs to move up on your priority list.

Ask yourself:

- Do I have a spiritual basis?
- How do I spend time developing my spirituality?
- In what ways do I ensure that I am centered?

Relationships

Your Relationship with Yourself

What have you done for you lately? As leaders, CEOs, and caretakers, you have many responsibilities and honestly a lot of people depend on you. In the midst of making sure you meet your deadlines, attend meetings, and cover all of your bases, it is important to make time and space to exercise self-care. I like to think of it as making breathing room in your life.

Self-care is not selfish and is vital to getting and staying focused. It is a good practice to press pause and do something that will replenish your mind, body, and soul. If you are a seasoned leader, you may have this all figured out already but reminders are good. We are even reminded during travel on airplanes.

Travel experts state that if you do not put your mask on within 30 seconds of the cabin pressure dropping, you are at risk of passing out. Imagine you have a child or elderly person with you who may need assistance. If you don't take care of your mask first, both of you are at risk of passing out. It is not different in life. Making sure you have oxygen first is key if you want to be alert and healthy enough to care for and lead others.

This hit home even further during a conversation while visiting with a friend at one of my favorite teashops. We were catching up and I explained to her how I had been working long hours and was exhausted most of the time, she lovingly told me, "Honey, you need to take care of yourself." I agreed with her, and then she asked the same question I posed to you earlier, "What do you do for you?" It may be time for you to evaluate your "me time."

"Me time" is the time you set aside to focus on yourself. Everyone needs "me time." Do something that brings you joy, fulfillment, and peace. That might be going to the movies, playing basketball, reading, working out, getting away, or simply resting.

25

Whatever it is, make and take the time for yourself, family, and friends will love you for it. You will love you for it! If time is your concern, schedule it in just like you do everything else. You are important, so do not make any excuses.

Prioritizing rest is a component of self-care that I must emphasize. The amount of sleep you get affects your memory, learning, mood, motivation, judgment, and perception. Research conducted at the University of Rochester Medical Center (URMC), revealed a system that drains waste products from the brain during sleep. Through several experiments on mice, researchers revealed that cerebral spinal fluid is pumped around the brain to wash out waste products – similar to how a dishwasher cleans dishes. Dr. Maiken Negergaard of URMC stated, "We sleep to clean our brains."

Former president Bill Clinton also understands the importance of rest. In an interview with Jon Stewart on the Daily Show, he discusses the effects of sleep deprivation on decision-making. When asked what advice he had for President Obama, he said, "In my long political career, most of the mistakes I made, I made when I was too tired, because I tried too hard and worked too hard. You make better decisions when you're not too tired. So that would be my only advice." That is great advice for any person.

Consider your cell phone. All day long you carry your phone to and fro. You use it constantly to text, talk, email, play games, and so on. At the end of the day, the battery is depleted from the day's use. The phone needs to be connected to a charger so the battery can replenish itself.

We are no different from our cell phones. You go back and forth talking, texting, emailing, meeting, running errands, making decisions, and the list goes on and on. At the end of the day, your battery- the brain- is depleted and needs recharging. You need rest in order to function properly the next day. The Creator himself took time to rest after his work. If rest is important to him, then it should be important to you.

Your Relationship with Others - Family & Friends

In his poem, "Mediation XVII", John Donne states "No man is an island, entire of itself; every man is a piece of the continent, a part of the main." He reminds us that we are not alone. Family, friends, and people are in your life for a reason.

We humans naturally adopt the thought patterns and actions of those we spend time with. The people in your inner circle contribute tremendously to who you are. It is said that you are the sum total of the five people you spend the most time with. There is a lot of truth to that idea. Examine who is in your inner circle. Are they adding to you? Are they taking away from you?

I have seen this principle play out in my own life. From childhood, I have loved books and reading. I attribute that to my parents and teachers who planted the seed for a love of books. They were consistently reading books, newspapers, and magazines. Now, just like them, I always have something to read at my disposal - in the bedroom, living room, and on my technology. Clearly, a book is never far from reach. This same love for literacy is something I hope to pass on one day to my children as it has been something extremely beneficial to me in my life.

Tomorrow is not promised to anyone. If you struggle to connect with family and friends, consider this. How do you want to be remembered when your eulogy is read? What legacy do you want to leave behind? Taking and making time to spend with those you love and care about will last for years to come.

Career

Work is a priority that provides you with resources to cover your expenses and enjoy your life. While you are at work, demonstrate excellence. Excellence simply means outstanding. You should stand out! Show up on time. Dress and act professionally. Follow the policies and procedures to the best of your ability. Contribute your ideas, gifts, and talents. You never know what doors can open up for you. Your gift will make room for you among great men.

Avoid workplace pitfalls like gossip, politics, backbiting, and time wasting. These will only drag you down, cause you to lose focus, and make you unproductive. While in any position, you should be useful, effective, and make a positive impact.

Takeaway

Having balance and exercising self-care is important to your overall health. Balance prevents burnout and helps you enjoy life. It starts with establishing priorities that include, but are not limited to, your spiritual life, relationship with yourself, relationship with others, and your career. Creating balance doesn't stop there. It takes knowing your capacity, setting boundaries, and planning. If you create and maintain balance, you will be a more productive person.

Reflect and Act:

1. Invest in yourself. Find resources (books, retreat, and/or training) that will help you spiritually and/or professionally.

2. Make a list of three "me time" activities and commit to having that time. Put them on your calendar and schedule away.

3. Laughter is good for the soul. Plan a family and/or friend game night. Eat, laugh, and have fun!

Capacity: Don't Crack

Are you beyond your limits?

One of the things I love about traveling out of the country is when I get an opportunity to stay at a resort. Besides the fabulous amenities, I have to admit I love the food buffets. From the beautiful native fruit to the array of sweets, it is any visitor's food heaven. If you haven't traveled outside of the US, they are very reminiscent of the local buffets with an international twist.

During one vacation, I got ahead of myself and put more on my plate than my stomach could handle. By the time I had taken four bites, I was almost full. My eyes were bigger than my stomach. Have you ever put more on your plate than you could chew?

Are you or have you been an over eater? Have you ever taken on or been assigned more responsibilities than what you seem to be able to handle? If you are a leader or manager, perhaps you have dished out too much or assigned too many tasks creating over eaters (overachievers) in your organizations. Having an overloaded plate will eventually lead to ineffectiveness if changes are not made.

Limits

We all have limits. If you want to stay focused and be productive, you must know and operate in your own capacity and limits. Leaders must go a step further and understand the capacity and limits of those they lead - what they can and cannot handle.

Consider three vessels we see frequently - a coffee mug, a bathtub, and a river. Each holds a different amount of liquid. Imagine trying to put the water from a bathtub into a coffee mug. It is not going to work! You will have what my mother calls a "grand mess." The same is true for we as humans. We are all different and can only do so much. There is a maximum amount of information that each of us can hold and a maximum amount of responsibilities or tasks we can manage effectively. Learn to honor and embrace your personal wiring.

Did you know that your brain has a certain capacity to retain information as well? Information overload, or cognitive overload, can lead to "analysis paralysis." Most of the time people get the same thing every time they go to a buffet. Why you may wonder. Besides gravitating to what they like, there are too many options. This is analysis paralysis at work. We don't know whether to get Cesar salad or chef salad. We struggle between the baked chicken or spaghetti and meatballs. Options are great, but there are times when too many options is a hindrance. As a result, we have the tendency to get what you have always gotten because it is safe.

31

In addition to analysis paralysis, going beyond your capacity can lead to hasty decision making. Disregard the fact that you do not even like Brussel sprouts, they end up on your plate because you just want to sit down and eat.

These problems occur within organizations far too often. Employees are guilty of signing up for too many tasks, and superiors are guilty of dishing out too many assignments. As a result, the organization suffers because overloaded individuals cannot be productive.

In order to avoid overload, there must be a serious evaluation of individual capacities. Consider the following.

1. What is the size of the container?

Leaders must accurately evaluate their own capacity and then the capacity of those they are leading. Observe how they are handling the responsibilities you have given them. Are they struggling or are they successful? Have you overloaded them? If they are struggling, make the necessary adjustments. Know when enough is enough.

2. What are the signs that you may have delegated too much?

You or your people are not being effective or neglect responsibilities. Sometimes neglect comes as a result of putting too much on their plate. There is much truth to the notion that "adding more water to the Kool-Aid only makes it weaker."

3. Do I create an open and honest environment for those on my team?

Do you give room in your organization for people to voice concerns? Individuals in or on your team should feel comfortable speaking up especially when they are overwhelmed. Great leaders learn to listen to their people and value their input.

Let's consider another facet of maintaining correct capacity. A container, or individual, does not need to be completely full. An empty space on a plate allows room for growth and expansion. When new assignments or opportunities arise, the individual with space in their container can gladly accept the responsibility. Next time you consider taking on another task or dishing out one, pause and ask yourself is it best to add to this plate right now.

<u>Takeaway</u>

Knowing your capacity and the capability of others on your team is important to ensuring that everyone is working to the best of their ability. We all have limits. Going beyond those limits is dangerous for you and your team. Evaluate yourself and your group. Make the necessary adjustments so that everyone can stay focused, be productive, and get the job done.

33

Reflect and Act:

1. Are you over capacity? Make a list of your priorities and responsibilities. Eliminate those things that are not a priority in this season of your life.

2. Evaluate your team. Have you dished out too many tasks to particular individuals? If so, how can you adjust this problem?

Sweet Spots

What do you have that the world needs?

Every now and then, I make my way to watch the Houston Astros play in Minute Maid Park. Baseball has always intrigued me – partially because I am trying to figure out the plays and partially because there have been many life lessons I have learned from what I do understand about the game. One of the best pieces of wisdom that speaks volumes to staying focused and being productive is the concept of a sweet spot.

In baseball, the sweet spot is the best place for the bat to make contact with the ball. When a ball hits a bat, the force causes vibrations. When a ball connects with a bat's sweet spot, you get the least amount of vibrations, which gives the maximum output and allows the ball to go its farthest. Just as a baseball bat has a sweet spot, people have sweet spots- areas that allow us to give our best.

It is important that you position yourself and the players on your team in their sweet spot. Sweet spots are those intersecting areas where we exhibit passion, ability, and add value to others. How do you know if you or your team is operating in your sweet spot? Consider the following criteria:

- Excitement - They are excited about it.
- Excellence - They excel at it.
- Effectiveness - They are highly effective in it.
- Experience – They have a great understanding of it
- Expense – If they had to, they would do it for free or people will pay them to do it.
- Expertise – They can do it "with their eyes closed"
- Esteemed – They are respected for it.

Your talents and personality factor into your sweet spot as well. It is no wonder why Steve Jobs excelled in his position. He was creative, passionate, and enjoyed getting into the minds of his consumers to produce the next innovative product. These products have changed how we communicate forever. Likewise, Oprah's business smarts and ability to connect with people from all walks of life led her to unprecedented success in the media industry. Her influence has globally shifted countless lives for the better. Think about your talents and your personality. Are you operating in your sweet spot?

Equally important to operating in your sweet spots is aligning yourself and your team to your goal(s). In other words, you want to ensure you properly position yourself and your team in order to reach your goals. For example, your extroverted, on time, task master would probably do the best job at helping you with customer service.

Alignment in an organization is comparable to the importance of wheel alignment on a car. When your tires are not going in the right direction, it affects your steering, safety, and durability. Chances of you safely reaching your destination are slim. It is no different on a team. If you are not properly positioned and aligned with the larger goal, it can compromise your ability to reach the intended end.

When the need for a new position or new challenge arises, you want to ensure that you choose the right individuals who will work hard to make sure plans are implemented well. Allowing people to operate in their sweet spot ensures maximum output among your team members.

Takeaway

Leaders should position themselves and their group members in their individual sweet spots. Sweet spots are those areas where we exhibit excitement, excellence, effectiveness, experience, expense, expertise, and value. Alignment to a goal is important to optimal focus and productivity.

Reflect and Act:

1. What is your organization's goal? Reflect on what positions you need in order to reach your goal. What adjustments do you need to make?

2. List all of the individuals in your organization and their sweet spots. Do the positions you currently have them in align with their sweet spots?

Double A Factor: Approach & Attitude

Do you need an attitude adjustment?

As a former elementary school teacher, I am no stranger to situations that require a   sound response. As you can imagine dealing with little people, there were often fires to put out that included homework checks, runny noses, test reviews, and minor recess conflicts to settle. In the midst of dealing with the fires, I had to maintain focus for myself and my team (my students) to ensure we were winning.

As a teacher, you never really know what hand you will be dealt for the year. Each year a different group brought in with them a different set of dispositions, talents, and challenges. In other words, your group may be easy going or they may come with lots of challenges. When I received an easy hand like a small class size, I cheered, celebrated, and was overall happy. The true test came when I had a challenge in my hand like a larger class size or students who were misbehaving.

Undesired behavior or under performance from someone on your team can test you but also lead you off course if not addressed. The key is making sure you have the correct attitude and approach for the given challenge in order to have the best outcome. It starts with self-awareness followed by people awareness and action.

Self-Awareness

Knowing your own personality and disposition is important to determining the proper approach to take when addressing something you are not satisfied with. If you are a no-nonsense type of person, consider seeking the assistance of someone who is better at connecting and talking to people. If you have difficultly giving feedback because you are laissez-faire, seek the assistance of someone who deals with confrontations head on. A state of balance should emerge.

"Attitude is a little thing that makes a big difference." As stated by Mr. Churchill, having a positive attitude is important in any situation you approach. Ninety percent of the time, a positive attitude leads to a positive outcome. Reflect on the way you think and feel about something or someone before you approach the situation. If you approach something with a negative attitude, chances are you will get what you expect- negativity. Diplomacy has always shown to be a great approach.

After reflecting on your attitude, consider your team, and start developing an action plan. Before making any moves, you must ask yourself three important questions:

- How is my attitude?

- How effective am I at giving feedback?
- Does my feedback lead to desired change?

People Awareness

Know the people you are dealing with. In my teacher role, the key to properly disciplining my students *was* my attitude and approach. My own attitude and actions determined whether the adjustments in a student's behavior was effective or not. Furthermore, building relationships with students and understanding their personalities helped me determine the correct approach. Have you taken time to truly learn the people in your organization? Do you know their history? How do they respond? This knowledge is invaluable when deciding your course.

My students ranged from shy and introverted to boisterous and extroverted. They all needed redirection and guidance, just in different ways. Here is an overview of the various approaches I took with my students. You may find something helpful in it as you consider responding to challenges and conflicts.

The Look- An intense glare was enough to straighten some students up. Once students saw "the look," they knew I meant business and straightened up immediately.

The Phone Call- These students needed a verbal and visual reminder that a parent, grandparent, aunt, uncle, or coach was only a phone call away if needed.

The Private Conversation – Some students needed private correction. I used a loving, but firm, approach. **I praised in public and protested in private**. I made sure they were very clear about what was expected of them and where they had not met the expectation. A majority of the time, these students were aware of what they did wrong. Having the conversation gave us the opportunity to get to the root of what went wrong and why it went wrong. It also gave me an opportunity to get them back on track. Interestingly, this approach worked with both introverts and extroverts.

Iron Fist – Some students were defiant. These students had issues with authority figures and complying with rules. With these students, I took the "iron fist" approach. Thankfully, this was far and few in between. I reminded them of my expectations in a straightforward manner without sugar coating. Consequences were tough, but this was the only way to successfully get their attention and correct their behavior.

Praise- Some students need to be caught doing right. Praising and giving them specific feedback always kept them on track. If Johnny was told, "I like how you are standing in line," to him that was a mental cue that he was standing in line properly. However, telling Johnny, "I like how you are standing in line with your feet together, hands behind your back, and facing forward," gave him more specificity when it came to what I was looking for. He knew exactly what my expectations were when it was time to line up. Praise generally works for all personalities as most people like to be complimented.

After self- awareness and people awareness, the next and final step is choosing the right approach.

Just as I had to take different approaches with my students, leaders must take different approaches with those on their team. Your team environment can be affected positively or negatively, depending on your skillset in navigating social dynamics.

Consider a leader who uses the *Iron Fist* approach with someone who is compliant and mild mannered. If this approach is taken, it could cause that individual to shut down completely and/or not process what is being said. In the same way, if a leader takes a less direct approach like *The Look* with someone who needs strict guidelines and direction, it is likely that no progress will be made.

Have you mismatched the approach and personality? Don't fret if you have. There are tools out there for fostering healthy relationships and stress the importance of actively guiding a team member to proper behavior and better performance. You do want to consider the values, your intentions, and the timing of your approach.

One thing I have noticed is that the underlying foundation of many of these resources is showing team members love, respect, and responsibility. These values have proven to be more effective in redirecting inappropriate behavior and has given then logical steps towards proper behavior.

Another thing to consider is approaching someone with heavy emotion or selfishness intent. Take time to step back, calm down, and process the challenge. People can discern your sincerity. If you are giving feedback to make yourself look better or only to make the other person look bad, it will eventually show. An impure motive creates distrust. Genuinely caring about the people on your team and having their best interest in mind will go a long way.

Keep in mind that timing is everything! Be mindful that potentially great and necessary feedback can be given at the wrong time and in the wrong tone. Likewise, poor feedback given at the right time may not yield the results you desire to see. This diminishes the opportunity of effective improvements.

If you have genuine concerns about someone's behavior or performance, be honest with them. You may be surprised at what you find out. Having a candid exchange with them (and not others) about where they are and where they need to be can be magically for your team. Create a plan together with action items so that they can reach their goal, offering as much coaching and counsel as needed (or willing) to get there.

Now, you may have push back and may be thinking, "I do not have time for that. My way is the right way, and

44

it's my way or the highway." Perhaps your way is the right way and you cannot make everyone happy. However, putting some time into getting to know yourself, your team, and using the right approach will ultimately benefit all in the long run, put you back on track, and facilitate your team's focus and productivity as you work to reach goals.

Takeaway

Engaging your team in order to have positive change hinges on your attitude and approach. It requires that you know yourself and those in your organization. That information will help you identify which approach to take in order to create positive results. Constructive feedback, taken with the right approach, will take you and others a long way in improving your cohesiveness, focus, and productivity.

Reflect and Act:

1. What type of approach do you normally take when giving feedback? Has it proven effective?

2. Have you used the wrong approach when handling a situation? If so, reflect on how you can use a   different approach to properly address the situation.

Recommended Readings:

Patterson, Grenny, McMillan, & Switzler. *Crucial Confrontations: Tools for Resolving broken promises, violated expectations, and bad behavior.*

Maxwell, John. *Attitude is the Difference Maker.*

Let's Talk

*Communication is like glue for relationships
and fuel for focus.*

When I was a little girl, occasionally I would watch the telenovelas (Spanish soap operas) and the news on Univision, a major Spanish – speaking channel. My mother would pass by the living room and ask "Ashley, do you even understand what they are saying?" "Yes, I do," I replied adamantly not really having a clue yet but knowing somewhere deep down that I would understand it. Back then, I did not quite understand my deep connection to the Spanish language but after having lived a little, it all makes sense. That initial interest sparked my quest to learn a language that has impacted my life in many ways.

I went on to take Spanish courses in middle school and high school. Later I would continue studies in college in Costa Rica and Nicaragua. I did not know then that I would be preparing to serve students who were bilingual. I also did not know then that I would be traveling to various Spanish speaking countries. Who else knows what the future holds, but what I do know is that had I not learned the language of the communities that I was in, I would have been in some deep trouble. Moreover, I would

47

not have been able to connect to the people. One thing I do understand and something we can all be reminded of is that communication is key to sustaining healthy, thriving relationships and critical to maintaining focus. Whether personal or professional, the art of encoding and decoding messages is something we all can work on in our quest to focus and become more productive.

There are many thoughts and opinions about communication – what it is, what it is not and whether it is truly important or not. For the sake of simplicity and the purpose of this text, communication can be simply defined as the exchange of thoughts, messages, or information, as by speech, signals, writing, or behavior.

We are bombarded daily with messages that impact our lives and can assist or impede our focus. Let's dig a little deeper into the benefits of communication, the consequences of poor communication, and some ideas for enhancing communication.

Benefits of Communication

There are major benefits when clear communication is in place between two parties. Whether in a personal setting with friends and family or in a professional setting, clear communication produces things that foster focus that include but are not limited to –

- More clarity, less confusion
- Healthy and mutually beneficial relationships

- Peace, which is priceless.
- Support
- Targeted Teamwork
- Productive Conflict (*Not all conflict is bad. If handled with tact and grace, disagreements can produce something better than anticipated.)

Consequences of Poor Communication

Focus can be impeded by lack of, frequently delayed, or no communication. These communication crises can lead to the manifestations of the following:

- Misunderstandings
- Worry
- Overthinking
- Uncertainty
- Poor teamwork

I experienced some of these manifestations through a minor communication crises. I often take much needed breaks from electronics and large social scenes in order to rest, relax, recharge, and rejuvenate. I typically inform those in my inner circle that I am going into shut down mode; but one time I forgot. My mother attempted to contact me and freaked out when she heard no response for two days. When I finally retrieved my phone, there were tons of missed calls and texts. I had to remind her that I was just in one of my shut down modes. In order to avoid alarming my mother or anyone else again, I make a conscious effort when I shut down to inform those close to me. This ensures that they do not worry about me.

I have also experienced the effect of lack of communication can have on teamwork. If proper communication is not present, roles and responsibilities will not be well defined. There is potential for tasks to overlap or be completely left out. I was once a part of a team in which responsibilities were not properly delegated. As a result, a team member was embittered because they were doing all the work. Coming together to work on any type of project was often met with tension from there on. These are the things you want to avoid for yourself or your team.

Enhancing Communication

While there is no magical solution, there are several skills that enhance communication. Communication is a two-way street. It is a dialogue between two parties. Being able to clearly and concisely tell your story or point of view in a situation is very important. If you struggle with clarity, try writing down what you want to say. Facilitating conversations is easier with a road map. This strategy has helped me tremendously in completing projects, assignments, and having difficult conversations.

Listening is an equally important skill and seems to be a lost art in our modern times. Diverse distractions and shortened attention spans have driven good listeners to near extinction. This is unfortunate, because active listening is a necessity for focusing, being productive, and having a successful team. Hopefully we can reclaim the much-needed skill.

Great listening starts with tuning out distractions and truly paying attention to whoever is speaking. ***Listen with the intent to understand and not to respond***. This can be hard. I get it, but the benefits are worth it. If the person is comfortable, take notes so you don't miss anything. This gives you time to process what was spoken. You can clarify that the information you received from the speaker was interpreted correctly.

Words are not the only vehicles of communication. Sometimes we overlook nonverbal cues like facial expressions, gestures, and body language. They are powerful and vary from community to community. A smile or thumbs up often communicates pleasure or approval, and folded arms and a scowl communicates displeasure or disapproval. Pay close attention to yourself and your team. What are you or they communicating non-verbally?

Thinking is the final essential skill that you need for proper communication. How you interpret what is being said or seen is critical. Before you jump the gun, take time to process what information is coming your way.

Some Other Communication Tips and Tricks

- Aim to respond to necessary emails or phone calls within 24- 72 hours.
- Use automated email response when needed (vacation, extended periods away room the office)
- Get creative with your communication by using oral, written, and non-verbal modes. Newsletters, call outs, social media, and even the bathroom stalls have been great ways to get a message across.
- Communicate with consistency and frequency.
- Be mindful of generational and gender differences in communicating. Learn from those younger and older than you. Women and men should also take time to learn from each other. Your goal is to connect with all and not to make anyone feel alienated. For example, some communicate via text for the sake of brevity while others prefer a phone call for connection.
- Understand the person(s) you are communicating with. As Steve Covey puts it, "Seek first to understand, then to be understood."

Takeaway

Communication is a critical and an important on-going process that will help you and your team stay focused and reach goals. Lack of communication often results in misunderstandings, worry, overthinking, uncertainty, and poor teamwork. Speaking, listening, and paying attention to non-verbal cues are vital to enhancing communication which impacts focus.

Reflect and Act:

1. Reflect on how well you communicate with your team or organization. If communication is lacking, survey your group to find out the communication styles that exist in your organization.

2. How well are you at responding? If you are bad at it, challenge yourself to respond to phone calls, texts, and/or emails within 24-48 hours.

3. Do you have an event or project coming up? Try implementing a new way of communicating to get the word out.

Recommended Readings:

Patterson, Grenny, McMillan, & Switzler. *Crucial Conversations: Tools for Talking When Stakes are High.*

Trust is a Must

Are you trustworthy?

When you sit down at a table to eat, you pull out a chair and sit in it. You do this without hesitation. You may check the sturdiness of it but ultimately you sit down without much reserve. In reality, the chair could collapse and you could fall to the ground. Regardless, you trust that the chair will hold you when you sit down.

One of my favorite leaders would often use this illustration of the trust we put in a chair as a way to inspire us to trust in a higher power. Regardless of your religious beliefs, this leader clearly pointed out that trust is essential to our very lives and well-being. It is a firm confidence in the integrity, ability, and character of a person or thing and it is **the foundation of all relationships and a key to getting and staying focused.**

Trust is so important that the motto, "In God We Trust," it is printed on the U.S. dollar bills and on the edge of U.S. coins. Have you given thought to how important trust is to your ability to focus and reach goals in your organization? If not, I encourage you to reflect on this

54

small, five-letter word that can make a tremendous difference in your focus and productivity.

Building Trust

Building trust is a crucial to personal and team focus. If trust exists amongst team members, the team is bound to thrive. It starts with establishing and building mutually beneficial relationships and is strengthened through actions and character.

First, let's talk relationships. Individuals respond better to those they have relationships with. I once asked a colleague to do a small task for me. Without hesitation, she said, "Absolutely, I can help you." We had a pleasant relationship and I helped her with some projects in the past; however, I received a big news flash when I told her who the task would benefit. Her entire demeanor changed.

"I thought I was doing this for you, not her." *Wow*, I thought. Unknown to me there was an element of distrust between the two from something in the past. That encounter plus my own experiences with trust eroding and building confirmed my thoughts about mutually beneficial relationships all vital to trust.

Your actions influence the quality of trust between you and those on your team as well. If you are a leader, people are watching you. They pay attention to whether you follow through and they observe how you behave in diverse situations. How do you handle pressure or conflict? Do you honor confidentiality? Your responses to these things impacts your team's trust level.

Trust is also built through character. Some character questions that often roll around in people's minds.

- Are you honest?
- Do have integrity?
- Do you keep your word?
- Are your motives pure?
- Are your intentions pure?
- Are you consistent, committed, and competent?

The importance of trust and character was brilliantly illustrated in Lee Daniel's movie, *The Butler*. The African American domestics who worked in the White House exhibited strong character and work ethic. Cecil Gaines, the main character, was a secret advisor to many of the presidents he served. He was trustworthy, reliable, and consistent. Mr. Gaines did not come packaged as your typical leader or advisor; however, he was powerful in his own right because he influenced mighty men in crucial times. They trusted his character and consequently his wisdom.

This trust concept if further researched by Dr. John Gottman of the *Greater Good.* He has completed extensive research on trust and betrayal. He highlights what he calls "sliding door" moments, interactions that have the potential to build or erode trust. If attention is given to a person in a time of difficulty then trust can be built as the individual interprets your concern in a positive way. If no attention is given, then trust is eroded. I have experienced first-hand myself. Make those sliding door moments count positively in your life.

If we truly want our teams to trust us and each other, there are some key character analyzing that we need to undergo. Providing safe spaces and judgement free zones is important for trust. Your team should have the space to make mistakes, be vulnerable, and receive assistance when needed. These all play a huge role we aim for focusing better and being more productive.

Losing Trust

Trust that takes months and years to nurture and build can be destroyed in a matter of seconds. Many factors can send trust flying out the window, but more often than not, trust is diminished by some act of betrayal or broken personal, business, or ethical contract.

Breeches in confidentiality erode trust quickly. Nothing is worse than someone spilling the beans after you confide in them. I once told a fellow leader some sensitive personal information. The following day, someone else came to me and told me everything I had discussed in confidence with the other person. The third party might as well have been in the room during the original conversation. You can probably guess the trust was diminished in that relationship as the information was intentionally shared in a negative way. There are moments when someone may unintentionally share information against your wishes. Gauge if this is the case or not and exercise grace where needed.

Unfair or deceitful business deals and motives will immediately destroy trust as well. When someone tries to or does deceive you, it can make your blood boil. When money is involved, this can go to another level. To add, if your team thinks you are dishonest, or catches you lying, it diminishes the chances of them confiding in you again. Avoid the pitfalls of losing trust and along with your focus. Honesty is the best policy.

Rebuilding Trust

If you recognize trust as an issue you have or your team has, the work begins with identifying the root of the issue. Identify the "why" so you can move on to the "what." The "why" is the what actually happened – the betrayal, lie, or breech. The "what" is the necessary action taken to repair a relationship so that all parties can refocus on the goal. There may be times when the issue is not why but who. (This is a hard reality, but true.) These situations require us to dig a little deeper in order to move forward.

Some Simple Steps to Rebuilding Trust

1. Identify the root.

2. Forgive if you were offended.

3. Offer a sincere apology and changed behavior if you did the offending.

4. Establish ways to rebuild the relationship. Be realistic and start small like completing a small task together. As time and efforts show that you or that person is trustworthy again, work up to something bigger.

As with anything, use good judgment and discretion in deciding whether you should move forward with rebuilding trust with an individual. In my opinion and experience, there are just some people you cannot and should not trust. You are better off focusing without some.

Takeaway

Trust is essential to maintaining focus. Trust can be built through relationships, actions, and character. It can be lost through dishonesty, unfair deals, and impure motives. It can be rebuilt by identifying the root and implementing actions to rebuild trust if and when necessary. Trust is key to staying focused.

Reflect and Act:

1. Is there a trust issue on your team? Identify the root and create a plan to address it.

2. Generate a list of people you trust. Identify what characteristics about them make them trustworthy. Aim to surround yourself with these types of people and exhibit those characteristics yourself.

Recommended Reading:

Leocioni, Patrick. *The 5 Dysfunctions of a Team.* Covey, Steve. *The Speed of Trust.*

Reverse Procrastination: Just Do It

Is procrastination killing your progress?

The school district I began my educational journey with adopted a web-based instructional program. As one of the persons responsible for campus usage, I needed administrative access in order to monitor program usage. I emailed the department head to see if he could assist. Typically, these types of requests can take days. However, the individual responded to my request within 5 minutes.

I was amazed and thanked him for his prompt response in replying to my email. He replied,

"No sweat. I am a reverse-procrastinator. If I don't reply immediately, I will totally forget and never reply. So, I've learned to just stop and reply for small things. Otherwise my to-do list gets out-of-control long.

This small nugget of wisdom offered that day shifted how I did things tremendously. It has proven to be instrumental to overcoming the silent assassin called procrastination.

Delaying the execution of an important task is not the best habit to have. Putting off tasks wastes time and creates unnecessary delays. Unfortunately, it is a common

61

struggle for many people. **Procrastination is the enemy to productivity**, but please let me help you put this nemesis to rest. It starts with understanding why you procrastinate.

Why People Procrastinate

1. *Stress* - When we feel overwhelmed by responsibilities and situations, we have a tendency to avoid completing a task.

2. *Lack of* - Being without can often paralyze us from moving forward with tasks, projects, or reaching goals.

   Motivation – The task is important but you are just not motivated to start or complete it. Your creativity is drained along with your interest.

   Skill – You desire to complete the task but lack the necessary ability to do so.

   Discipline- You know what to do and how to do it but you lack the self-control to do it.

   Time Management- You don't know how to properly budget and/or manage your time.

   Organization- You are disorganized and all over the place. Everything is everywhere.

Resources- You are ready to complete the task but lack the fundamental resources to complete it. Resources include but are not limited to supplies, manpower, or money.

3. *Fear* - Fear is being in a constant state of anxiety or concern. An individual may procrastinate because they are afraid of completing something. The fear that leads to procrastination manifests itself in different ways.

Perfectionism- You put off completing something because you fear it will not be perfect.

Performance Anxiety – You are wary of falling short of set expectations – whether self-imposed or from others.

Failure- Fear of failure ranked #4 in a Gallup poll of top ten fears. You may find yourself procrastinating to avoid disappointment.

Rejection- The fear of finding out that you're not wanted may lead to procrastination.

4. *Laziness* - Laziness says, "I can, but I won't." There are times that one must admit that they are simply lazy about completing tasks. The issue is not stress, fear, or lack. The individual simply does not want to work. This mindset is erroneous, and it feeds procrastination.

5. *Adrenaline Junkies* - In this context, adrenaline junkies are those who enjoy the rush of completing tasks last minute. Maybe your best work emerges under pressure. The bottom line is that you enjoy the rush and often will create these types of situations. In this case, your procrastination is extremely intentional or just habitual.

6. *Fatigue* - When you are tired, there is a tendency not to want to do anything. Some battle with chronic fatigue syndrome which makes matters worse. If you are amongst this group, a few changes to your diet, exercise, and lifestyle can assist.

Ways to Overcome Procrastination

1. *Exercise the 2-minute rule.* If it takes less than two minutes to complete, do not add it to your to-do list. Just do it- plain and simple.

2. *Set deadlines.* Setting deadlines gives an end to your task or goal. Working with a timeline will help keep you on target.

3. *Create an action plan.* An action plan outlines the smaller, necessary tasks needed to complete a larger project, goal, or vision. Make a list of the tasks you have to complete. Prioritize your list by date and tackle the list one step at a time.

4. ***Get an accountability partner.*** Just as there is safety in numbers, there is accountability in numbers. Working with a partner or group on anything from exercise to your career fosters more commitment than going solo. Being accountable to an outside party will help you avoid procrastination. Find a strong individual(s) that you can check in with for progress.

5. ***Learn the Power of 30 minutes.*** Pastor Tommy Barnett has a life-changing concept called the Power of the Half Hour. Planning various thirty minutes spurts of devoted task tackling will make a huge difference. Setting aside 30 minutes to develop spiritually (e.g. prayer, reading, meditation) and physically (e.g. 30- minute walk, run, or workout) inevitably leads to desired results.

6. ***Be Proactive and Plan*** Planning is key to overcoming procrastination. Make a plan and stick with it. Make adjustments only as needed.

Takeaway

Procrastination kills progress and focus. It is the enemy of vision, focus, and productivity. People procrastinate for many reasons. For every reason people procrastinate, there is a solution to overcome it.

Reflect and Act:

1. If you struggle with procrastination, identify the reasons why you struggle. Don't overlook this step in your pursuit to end procrastination.

2. Find an accountability partner. Inform your partner about a task, project, or goal you desire to complete. Start your journey to completion by setting a deadline and creating an action plan.

Recommended Readings:

Barnett, Tommy. *The Power of the Half Hour.*

Consistency is Key

Are you stable, reliable, and dependable?

E every so often, there is an occasion that prompts people to work out like they never have before. While we should be proactive and exercise good personal well-being, it often takes events like weddings, class reunions, breakups, or the health scares to push us to take better care of their bodies.

It's no secret that if we are consistent with our workouts and eating habits, then we will stay on track to reach whatever fitness goals we have. I once lost 20 pounds in month preparing for a big event. How did I do it? The process was simple. I worked out everyday day for 30 minutes and traded the unhealthy parts of my diet for things that were better for my health – more fruits, vegetables, juicing, and less meat. Consistency is key to staying focused, being productive, and reaching your goals.

What exactly is consistency?

Consistency is always acting or behaving in the same manner. It is freedom from variation or contradiction. It is doing something a certain way all the time. Routine.

Repetition. However, you coin it, and whether or not you like it, it is important to maintaining focus and reaching goals. I must highlight that there are times when there is a need to embrace a change or something new; however, individuals in your organizations need to know that they have a leader and environment that is stable, reliable, and dependable.

What does consistency look like within an organization?

Character - When leaders are consistent in character and behavior, focus is maintained. If part of your character is honesty and excellence, individuals will expect honesty and excellence every time you are a part of something.

Communication - Great leaders have a consistent way of communicating with those they are leading. This may be a set meeting on a particular day of the week or weekly conference call. Whatever format, the routine serves as a vessel of stability on your team, ensuring that everyone is on the same page.

Commitment - Consistency and commitment go hand in hand. Consistency requires you and your team staying committed to the process of seeing a vision unfold.

What do I do if I struggle with consistency?

Consistency starts with discipline. **Discipline is not a dirty word.** It simply refers to a structured way   of completing tasks. If you work out, you understand results only come through consistent exercise. You cannot expect to look your best if your workout routine is inconsistent. Results may be there for a little while, but soon you will start to see your body back into the shape you were trying to run from. When that happens, it is time to get back at it again. Here are some ways to develop discipline.

- Start small and then expand.

- Keep you goal before you and post it in a space that will allow you to see it daily. Visuals work.

- Operate by what you know and not what you feel. Feelings are fickle and can sometimes deter us from reaching goals. You may not feel like holding your Monday meeting, but you know it is important to ensuring communication is constant. You may not feel like working out, but you know you should to lose weight.

Another important component of consistency is effort. If you want anything to work, you must put forth the effort. Your attempts must be determined. Do not wait until someone taps you on your shoulder. Get up and try. You will surprise yourself, which will prove to motivate you even more. Consistency creates stability, reliability, and dependability. You and your team will benefit, flourish, and be more productive when consistency is present.

<u>Takeaway</u>

Consistency is key to productivity. It is reflected in character, communication, and requires commitment. If you struggle with consistency, developing discipline and putting forth effort are essential. Consistency will prove to be beneficial to you and your organization.

<u>Reflect and Act:</u>

1. Reflect on the three areas of consistency-character, communication, and commitment. In which of the three areas are you most inconsistent? Identify the obstacles that contribute to the inconsistency. Determine one thing you can do differently to combat that obstacle.

2. Create a visual of your goal and post it where you can view it daily.

3. Find an accountability partner that is strong in the areas where you are weak. Ask them to help you in your quest to become consistent.

No is a Complete Sentence

Saying no is critical to maintaining focus.

"No is a complete sentence." A friend told me this when we were discussing an opportunity I turned down. I was asked to lead a project for a volunteer organization and I declined with a simple, "No thank you." A brief wave of guilt hit me. I always came through for this group and they knew they could depend on me. However, with the load I was carrying between work and my graduate studies, it did not take much time for me to realize I could not do it and preserve my sanity. Of course, the individuals who asked were a bit disappointed because I always willingly said yes. I, on the other hand, was completely satisfied in knowing that another responsibility was not added to my plate.

Have you ever been in a position where you knew you should say no and didn't or struggled saying no? Perhaps you have been asked to take on a project or extra commitment or maybe someone wants to borrow money. Whatever the situation may be, use good judgment. This may be a challenge for people pleasers, but if you know that the answer should be no, say no. If you struggle with saying no, you can take steps toward improvement.   The key to mastering the art of saying no is to understand why, when, and how to do so.

Why Saying No is Important

1. *It allows you to stay focused on your current priorities and your goals.* When I said no to the above-mentioned project, I was in graduate school. School was one of my top priorities. Saying yes to that project would have pulled my focus away from my studies.

2. *It helps you to maintain balance in your life.* Balance is important. If I had agreed to the project, I would have been saying no to rest and much needed me time.

3. *Saying no allows you to say yes to the right priorities and people.* Saying no and disappointing some people frees you up to say yes to the right people. There are times when saying no to others means saying **YES to you**. It will help you choose your obligations wisely.

When to Say No

1. *When what is being asked of you does not align with your priorities, vision, goals, or values.* When I was asked to lead the project, my priority and goal was to complete graduate school.

2. *When what is being asked of you exceeds your capacity.* The project required time, energy, and   effort.

Phone calls, planning, meetings, and decision- making were all a part of the equation. Taking the task on would have put me over my limits mentally and physically.

3. ***When your reality does not support what is being asked of you.*** If someone asks you to lend them a large amount of money and your bank account (your reality) does not support that request, then the answer is no.

How to Say No

1. ***Keep it simple and straightforward.*** Less is more. You do not need to do a bunch of explaining. I simply told those who asked me, "No thank you. I have commitments that I'm focused on right now."

2. ***Be mindful of your words and tone.*** What you say and how you say it matters. What you communicate can be misinterpreted if you are not careful. Keep in mind that there may be times when you have to be more assertive than usual. These instances should be minimal if expectations have been set.

3. ***Establish expectations & limits.*** The more you let people know up front, the easier it will be for you to say no and for them to understand your decision.

When to Say Yes

1. ***When What is asked of you aligns with your priorities, vision, goals, and values.***

73

2. *When the benefits outweigh the costs*

3. *When the time is right* Timing is everything. The right thing at the right time will often produce great results.

Takeaway

Remember that no is a complete sentence. Knowing why, when, and how to say no is critical to maintaining focus. There will be times, however, that you can and should say yes to opportunities or decisions that come your way. Yes, may be the right answer if the question aligns with your vision, goals, and values. No is one of the many words that will keep you focused and on the road to greater productivity.

Reflect and Act:

1. Practice saying no with a friend or family member. Take a deep breath and let out a loud "NOOOOO!"

2. Is there currently something you know you need to say "no" to? If so, determine when and how you will do it.

Recommended Readings:

Cloud, Henry. *Boundaries: When to Say Yes, How to Say No to Take Control of Your Life.*

Part III: Other Focus Factors

What's the Plan?

When you fail to plan, you plan to fail.

I attended a coed game night where we played, *Gestures*. It was the highlight of our night. If you have never played *Gestures*, imagine high-speed charades. Participants are responsible for acting out phrases without talking. In return, their teammates have to guess the phrase they are acting out. There are different color cards, blue or red, which have different point values, one and three respectively. During our competitive game of guys versus girls, we all had one goal in mind and that was to win.

During the game, people incorporated some intriguing strategies. Some stuck to the one-point words which were easier to perform, while some used the difficult three-point words. Others chose a combination of the two.

The men had the tendency of sticking to the one-point cards or deciding as they went along. The female team rallied together and decided to use a combination of one and three point cards. This gave the female team more points and put them in the lead. Some of the men took noticed this and adjusted their strategy to match the women's strategy. In the end, the ladies, who planned ahead, took home the *Gestures* crown that evening.

This simple game of *Gestures* highlights the benefits of planning. If you want to accomplish a goal and achieve victory, you must plan. Planning involves assessing a situation and then setting goals. The goal of *Gestures,* as with most games, is to win. Planning starts here. Strategies must be developed and monitored. Then, they must be evaluated to determine their degree of success or failure. There is a simple process that can help you plan. Whether the project is small or large, this process can help you focus and achieve your goals.

Step 1: *Assess Situation*

Ask yourself two simple questions: What do I see? What does this mean? Given the *Gestures* scenario, there were two teams with the same objective and only cards, a timer, and imagination at their disposal.

Step 2: *Determine Goals*

Steve Covey, author of *Seven Habits of Highly Effective People*, tells us to begin with the end in mind. This step helps you determine what you are trying to accomplish. For the *Gestures* games, everyone's goal was to win- nothing more, nothing less. The next step was to work backwards from that goal to figure out a strategy.

Step 3: *Determine Strategies*

This step is critical. This is where the action happens. For our *Gestures* showdown, the guys decided to go with the simple, consistent one-point words, whereas the ladies decided to go with the combination strategy.

In this step, you determine what you are going to do to reach your goal step by step. You decide the who, what, when, and where of each strategy. Each component is vital to making the strategy happen. Establishing deadlines is also important. Deadlines eliminate procrastination, provide a sense of urgency, and keep you on track to reaching your goals. Just be mindful to set realistic deadlines.

Step 4: *Monitoring Strategies*

"What gets monitored gets done." There is much truth to the old adage. Monitoring not only makes sure things get done but also gives you the opportunity to see if something is, or is not working. Most teachers will tell you that, if homework is not getting checked, then the students will not complete it.

Monitoring of a strategy or system can determine your success or failure. If a strategy is not working, then adjustments should be made. For example, at some point in our game of *Gestures,* some of the men changed their strategy. They acted out three - point word cards or a combination of one and three points.

Step 5: *Evaluation and Reflection*

After the plan has been executed, it is time to determine whether the strategy worked. Ask yourself and your team what could be done differently next time. The SWOT Analysis is a great tool for evaluation and reflection. (It can also be used before in the assessment phase.)

Developed by Albert Humphrey while working for the Stanford Research Institute, the SWOT analysis stands for Strengths, Weaknesses, Opportunities, and Threats (or Tensions). Strengths are aspects of a project that were beneficial, helpful, and good. Weaknesses are aspects that were harmful or unfavorable. Opportunities are those areas where there is room for growth. Finally, threats or tensions are issues that can cause trouble.

An alternative to a SWOT analysis is the Glow and Grow analysis. Glows are areas that worked well. Grows are areas where there is room for improvement in the future.

Here are some other planning pointers that can help you achieve your day-to-day, short term, or long-term goals.

• **Always plan your priorities**. Remember the chapter on balance and self-care? Just as you plan meetings, you must plan your priorities - spiritual   time, me time, date nights, and family time. You should even plan planning time.

- **Long Term Planning** - Long term planning requires vision mapping for the future. Perhaps you are planning to build wealth or establish a business. This will also require setting goals, monitoring, evaluating, and a large amount of perseverance. Rome was not built in a day.

- **Short Term Planning** - Perhaps you have a short-term goal like finishing school or getting out of debt. These short-term goals can be reached quickly but require more frequent monitoring to make sure you are on track.

- **Weekly Planning**- Consider mapping out your meetings and leisure activities for the week. If you maintain a household, planning meals will be a great help to you and can even be cost effective. It may seem tedious but it is helpful.

- **Daily Planning**. At the end of your day, reflect on the progress made and make plans for the next day. It will make the start of your next day easier. For example, you realize that a few items on your to-do list did not get accomplished. Do not stress out. If your schedule permits, transfer them to tomorrow.

While making all of your plans, keep in mind that life happens. We get interruptions and things do not always go as planned; however, it is better to have a plan than to not have one at all.

Takeaway

Planning is an important component of staying focused. The five-step process of assessing, goal setting, determining strategies, monitoring, and evaluating can assist you in achieving victory. it is better to have a plan than no plan at all.

Reflect & Act:

1. Write down a goal you have (personal or professional). Create a list of strategies (action plan) to help you achieve that goal.

2. Construct a vision board to help you keep the goals you have set before you.

3. Have a project or event coming up soon? Use the SWOT or Glow/Grow analysis to evaluate before and after.

Smooth Transitions: Adjusting to Change

Are you ready to shift your mindset, perspective, & behavior?

I have recently transitioned from working in the public-school system to being fulltime entrepreneur and founding a non-profit. It has been no easy thing but extremely rewarding. Going from a set schedule to a flexible one has had its share of advantages and challenges. It requires that I exercise extreme intentionality when it comes to my schedule and how I manage my time. This transition like many of life's transitions come with making and adjusting to change.

Transitions occur all the time. In the home, they are subtle, but continuously happening. Babies are born, and they transition from crawling to walking to running. In a flash, children become teenagers working their way through the academic journey. Some continue to college. Those children leave their homes as adults and get married. Middle aged working adults transition into retirement and into a more seasoned life. In organizations, transitions are constantly happening as well. Promotions are given. Companies merge. People are hired, fired, and retire. Things are constantly changing.

Adjusting to life's changes can take a while to get adjusted to, but it does not have to be a daunting task. In fact, the only thing constant in life is change so you may as well make the best of it.

Change requires that you adopt a new mindset, perspective, and behavior. Whether you are an employee being promoted to an executive position, or a single person getting married, there are several keys to transitioning smoothly.

Be Prepared

Preparation will ease some of the tension caused by change. Do your homework. Seek counsel from someone who's been successful in the place you're headed to. Finding a mentor, engaging in personal and professional development, and researching, are several ways you can prepare for a transition. If you desire your own business, find a successful businessperson to glean wisdom from. Take some business courses and research everything about the sector of business that interests you.

In addition to doing your homework, create a plan. (See chapter *What's the Plan?)* Having a plan will help you during the various stages of your adjustment. After you make your plan, adjustments may be frequent, but remember, it is better to have a plan than to not have one at all.

Sometimes, change happens suddenly, and you will not have time to prepare. For example, you are placed in a new position after someone is unexpectedly fired, resigns, or is promoted. In situations like this, you must respond quickly. While feeling your way through the new position, seek guidance and counsel. Experience is one of the best teachers.

Be Positive

Approach change with as positive of an attitude as you can. You will often get what you expect, so expect the best. If you expect positive change and adopt a positive mindset, then you are more likely to have a better experience.

There *will* be bumps in the road. Life happens. However, an optimistic mindset will allow you to adjust quickly. As it is said, **"life is 10 % what happens to you and 90 % how you respond."** Your response to change is the key to success or failure.

Angela Duckworth exemplifies the role that optimism plays in transitioning. After transitioning from a career in management consulting to educating seventh graders in New York City, Duckworth was intrigued and inspired by her students. Realizing that her smartest students were not always successful, she began a quest to answer two questions. Who was successful and why were they successful?

With these two questions in mind, Duckworth left the classroom to perform research fulltime at the University of Pennsylvania. She and her research team studied rookie teachers, West Point cadets, and participants in the National Spelling Bee, to predict who would come out on top. They determined that the significant predictor of success was grit.

In Duckworth's own words, "grit" is a passion and perseverance to work towards a goal. It is stamina, a stick-with-it attitude, and not giving up easily. It is a perspective that life is a marathon and not a sprint. It is the proclivity to bounce back after adversity, challenges, or setbacks.

Just like these students, having tenacity and grit will help you remain positive in the face of transitions. My own grit has been developed in the midst of my career transition.

Be Clear

Change dredges up nervous questions and uncertainty. When in doubt, ask questions. So many questions go unanswered because people fear what others will think if they do not appear knowledgeable about subject matter. Take the risk of asking. Later, you will be grateful that you risked looking silly for a brief moment when you reap the rewards.

During transitional phases, be clear about your needs, feelings, and expectations. Communication is essential to success in your new position or status. Whether you have feelings of apprehension or excitement, you need to divulge them. Being upfront will settle the minds of all parties involved. Develop a clear view of the expectations placed upon you, and clearly voice the expectations you have for others. If you received a promotion, find out if you'll be working longer hours, or if you'll be receiving a raise. Clarity can lessen potential conflict and ensure that issues are not caused by a lack of understanding.

This brings to mind a great example of how lack of clarity and expectation can lead down a bad road. A few years ago, I attended a leadership conference where Dr. Samuel Chand spoke about the importance of setting clear expectations and meeting them. He stated that the distance between expectations and reality is conflict. The greater distance between them, the greater the conflict. To illustrate this, he used the example of a wife expecting her husband to come home at a certain time.

In his illustration, the husband tells his wife he will be home at 7:00 PM (expectation) but he shows up at 7:15 PM (reality). There is only a difference of 15 minutes between the two, which is not very much time. That could be due to traffic or a minor delay. The wife may not think twice about it. Consider the same husband who tells his wife he will be home at 7:00 PM (expectation), but then shows up at 8:00 PM (reality). The difference here is an hour. Perhaps the husband has a justifiable reason – stuck in traffic or stopping at the grocery store. His wife will likely question his whereabouts but not be angry upon his explanation. Now, consider the same husband who has told his wife he would be home by 7:00 PM (expectation) but shows up at 10:00 PM (reality). The difference here is three hours. The three-hour delay will have his wife on high alert and prompt her to ask many questions. A lot can happen in three hours. In this case, the conflict may be much greater. Clarity and communication is important.

Be Flexible

"Blessed are the flexible for they will not be bent out of shape." Having flexibility during transitions is essential. It takes time to adjust to new situations, environments, and ways of doing things. Practice patience with yourself and those around you. It is okay if you aren't 100% comfortable in the beginning of your transition. Ease and familiarity come with time.

I truly believe in "planned flexibility." It was a must in education and is certainly a must as an entrepreneur. I have learned to leave breathing room in my plans. Flexibility makes one more responsive to change. Consider this anecdote as you assess your own flexibility in new situations.

A captain of a ship received a message one night, "Change your direction 15 degrees north to avoid collision. A little indignant, the captain replied, "I am the captain of a large ship and recommend you change your direction 15 degrees south." The captain received the reply, "We are a light house."

Adjustments are a part of everyday life. Being flexible makes the adjustments much more manageable.

Some Pitfalls to Smooth Transitions

- *Being negative* - Negativity is toxic and will only bring you and others down. Find the best in the situation and harness your focus there.

- *Making assumptions*- Assume nothing. Ask questions and get the facts.

- *Being rigid* – The *Tao Te Ching,* an ancient Chinese text, states that whatever is flexible and flowing will tend to grow, whatever is rigid and blocked will tend to die.

- *Lack of interest or passion*- If you are not interested, or have no desire to transition, then you are likely to not give it the time or energy it needs to be fruitful.

Takeaway

Life is full of change. Transitions occur in our organizations, homes, and lives on a daily basis. Being prepared is the key to transitioning smoothly. Make an effort to be positive, clear, and flexible. Avoid the transitional pitfalls of negativity, rigidity, and assumptions. If you do these things, you are well on your way to a smooth transition.

Reflect and Act:

1. Are you currently facing a transition? Do you need more assistance in any of these areas - being prepared, being positive, being clear, or being flexible.

2. Identify an individual(s) that is strong in one of the areas you are currently struggling with and seek their counsel.

3. Reflect on a bumpy transition you experienced. Identify which pitfall made that transition bumpy. Develop a plan for how you can overcome potential bumpy transitions.

Recommended Readings:

Johnson, Spencer. *Who Moved My Cheese?*

M&Ms: Mentor-Mentee Relationships

Who are you passing the baton to?

Mentoring is a step in the right direction, a listening ear, and a nudge when you need it. Mentoring has been something that has proven to be purposeful in my life. I had been on both sides of mentoring – as the mentor and mentee. From both perspectives, I have had my share of mentoring success and failures. Through all of my experiences, I cannot deny that I have learned what to do, what not to do, and most importantly the value of human connection.

One of my favorite mentor-mentee pair is Socrates and Plato. They illustrate what I believe to be the ultimate function of an M& M relationship and how M&Ms (mentor-mentee relationships) should work. Most known for laying the foundation for western philosophy, Socrates was a bold and gifted scholar in Athens (470- 399 BC). In today's society, he is most known for introducing us to a style of teaching called the Socratic Method. His love of learning led him on a quest to discover truth. In his search, he concluded, "As for me, all I know is that I know nothing…Only God is wise.

Much of Socrates' teachings were condemned by the leaders of his time. He was criticized with "corrupting the youth" and believing in false gods. He was brought to trial and eventually executed in 470 BC.

Although his life was taken, his legacy was passed on through his famous mentee and student, Plato. Many of Socrates' teachings are recorded in the writings of Plato such as the *Apology of Socrates.* Taking the wisdom imparted to him by Socrates, Plato continued the pursuit for knowing and living truth. He founded the Academy, the first known institution of higher learning and continued his writings and teachings until his death.

This M&M pair confirms that the knowledge and experience mentors have serves to guide those starting out. They are pivotal to being able to focus in the right direction. Mentors coach, provide feedback, and speak for their mentees. They are great sounding boards for how to handle situations and, above all, they model behavior for those under their counsel.

In great M&M relationships, there is always an exchange. Lessons and wisdom are imparted on both ends. Socrates poured his knowledge into Plato. In return, Plato recorded Socrates' teachings on paper. Prior to Plato's writings, there were no written accounts of Socrates' teachings. With the passion Socrates instilled within him, Plato founded a learning institution where the quest for understanding, truth, science, and life on a deeper level continued.

Perhaps you are a mentor, mentee, or both. These relationships are priceless. It is no wonder many organizations have systems in place that facilitate them. If your organization does not have a system in place, these relationships can be easily implemented on an informal level. There are some essentials when it comes to mentor-mentee relationships.

- **Connection**. There should be a connection between the mentor and mentee. It could be the same line of work or aspiration.

- **Area of Expertise**. Typically, the mentor is better in a certain area than the mentee. The mentor teaches the mentee valuable lessons. The mentor should help mentees maximize strengths and navigate weaknesses. As mentioned before, the mentee can likewise teach the mentor in certain areas.

- **Integrity and Honesty**. Mentors should operate with integrity and good intentions. Giving sound, constructive feedback will help the mentee move forward while celebrating their small and large successes. On the other hand, mentees should be teachable. It's difficult to coach someone who thinks they know it all. If you knew it all, you wouldn't need a mentor.

- **Accountability**. Mentors and mentees assist each other in being response-able.

- **Time.** Mentors should pour everything they have into their mentees during the time they are connected.

Passing the Baton

It is important for all leaders to recognize and know when their time to lead in a specific capacity has passed. This does not mean the leader has to step down completely, but what it does mean is that a leader accepts their limitations (age, passion, or vision) and prepares a successor. When this is realized, developing a succession plan is necessary.

While working at Apple, when Steve Jobs' health took a turn, he realized it was time to step down. He gave control over to Tim Cook while retaining the title of executive chairman. He stated, "I look forward to watching and contributing to its [Apple's] success in a new role." His presence and counsel was still there, but the daily operations and decision-making were in the hands of Apple's new leader, Cook. Jobs knew that preparing the next leader was and is key to ensuring that legacies are established, gifts and talents are passed down, and organizations continue to focus and meet their goals.

Takeaway

These divine relationships are important to individuals, organizations, and even causes. Fostering and maintaining these relationships is not as hard as it may seem. Essentials to foster a great M& M relationship are connection, area of expertise, integrity and honesty, accountability, and time. You never know if your M&M relationship can change the world as Socrates and Plato's relationship did.

Reflect and Act:

1. If you don't have a mentor and believe it is time for one, brainstorm a list of potential mentors.

2. What other criteria do you believe are necessary for mentor- mentee relationships?

3. Have you done something nice for your mentor? An attitude of gratitude will go a long way.

Fit and Focused

S o much of our focus and productivity is connected to our wellness – mind, body, and soul. I would like to share with you some quick health solutions to help you stay focused and on track to becoming a more productive.

Focus & the Body

- Exercise at least 30 – 45 minutes a day (at least 3 - 4 times a week).

- Get a good night's rest

- Observe the Sabbath. Truly take one day to rest.

- Get a massage. They have extensive healing benefits.

- Stretch

- Mediate for at least 10 minutes a day.

- Essential oils are great for your body and environment – Rosemary, Peppermint, or Chamomile

Foods that Feed Focus[ii]

Blueberries

High in antioxidants that have shown to fight inflammations and improve brain functions.

Green Tea

Green tea contains caffeine and l'theanine, which both keep you alert.

Yogurt

Great for breakfast or as a snack, yogurt has probiotics, or "good bacteria" that helps promote digestive health.

Salmon

This fish is full of omega 3 fatty acids that help slow cognitive decline.

Eggs

This great protein has choline which is vital for brain development.

Leafy Greens

Popeye was onto something. Leafy greens like kale, spinach, and collards help slow cognitive decline and promote brain health.

Dark Chocolate

This treat is actually a stimulant which can give you a much-needed energy boost similar to a cup of java.

Final Focus Thoughts

Focus is key to leading a productive life and ensuring that you reach your goals. When you are able to conquer the distractions that try to conquer your, you win!

Identify those distractions and things that hinder you from focusing forward. Try one thing from the focus factor and get to work implementing something that will allow you to get and stay focus

Acknowledgments

My gratitude is extended to the many individuals I have meet along the way in my pursuit   to become the best version of myself - my village of family, friends, associates, and strangers I have meet along the way.

My biggest gratitude is extended to the Big Man who has allowed me to partner with him to positively impact the world.

About the Author

Educator, author, and leader, Ashley Martin, lives by the philosophy that "you learn something new every day." Serving students and adults, Ashley blends her love for educating, encouraging, and empowering others into dynamic conversations, sessions, and speeches. She is on a mission to help others become the best versions of themselves.

Ashley Martin is a New Orleans native. She holds a B.A. in Psychology from Scripps College (Claremont, CA) and a Masters of Educational Leadership from the University of St. Thomas (Houston, TX). Ashley resides in the Houston metro area but considers herself a global citizen.

Website: www.iamashleym.com

Email: info@iamshleym.com

Connect on Social Media Platforms

@ashleym3710

References

D avid Rock. *Your Brain at Work: Strategies for Overcoming Distractions.* New York City, NY: Harper Business, 2009.

Medina, John. *Brain Rules.* Edmond, WA: Pear Press, 2014.

NCDC (2005). Hurricane Katrina: National Oceanic and Atmospheric Administration. National Climatic Data Center

Pickert, Kate. "The Art of Being Mindful. "Time. February 3, 2014.
Lighthouse Fable. Bank of Ideas (Fables).

Electronic References

[i] https://www.babycentre.co.uk/a6752/your-childs-brain-a-visual-guide
[ii] http://www.chopra.com/articles/12-foods-to-help-you-focus#sm.0000pwpjxa193fetrzzfpsgqsbsvk

Positive Affirmation Decals

https://www.etsy.com/shop/MirrorMiracles

9 780990 770145